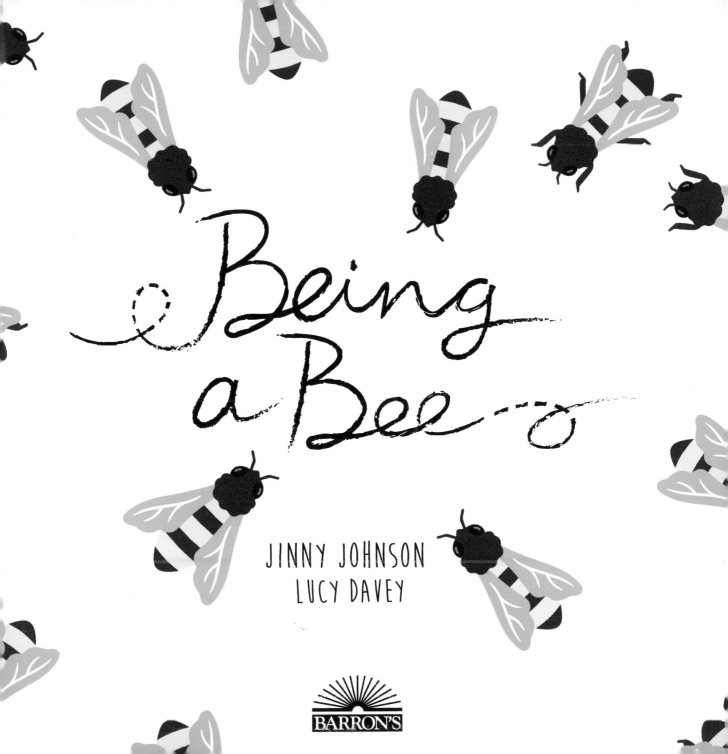

Being a Bee

JINNY JOHNSON
LUCY DAVEY

BARRON'S

First edition for the United States and Canada published in 2018 by Barron's Educational Series, Inc.

First published in 2017 by Wayland, an imprint of Hachette Children's Group
Part of Hodder and Stoughton, Carmelite House
50 Victoria Embankment, London EC4Y 0DZ

Design by Claire Yeo
Edited by Elizabeth Brent

All inquiries should be addressed to:
Barron's Educational Series
250 Wireless Boulevard
Hauppauge, NY 11788
www.barronseduc.com

ISBN: 978-1-4380-1117-2

Library of Congress Control Number: 2017935229

Date of Manufacture: December 2017
Manufactured by: WKT Co., Ltd., Shenzhen, Guangdong, China

Printed in China
9 8 7 6 5 4 3 2 1

Contents

Buzz, buzz, buzz

It's a sunny summer's day, and bees are
busy flying from flower to flower.

A bee is a kind of insect. It has three pairs of legs
and two pairs of wings, which move so fast
they make a buzzing noise.

There are thousands of different kinds of bees, but the bees we are going to talk about in this book are honey bees.

The honey bee's hairy body is covered in yellow and black stripes, warning other animals not to get too close. Female bees have a stinger at the end of their body and will use it to defend themselves and their family.

WATCH OUT —
a bee sting can hurt!

Meet the family

Honey bees live together in big families, called colonies.

The colony is home to the queen bee and as many as 50,000 worker bees. They build the nest, look after the young bees, and gather nectar and pollen from plants. All of the worker bees are female.

There are also some male bees in the colony.
They are called drones, and their job is to
mate with queen bees from other hives.

7

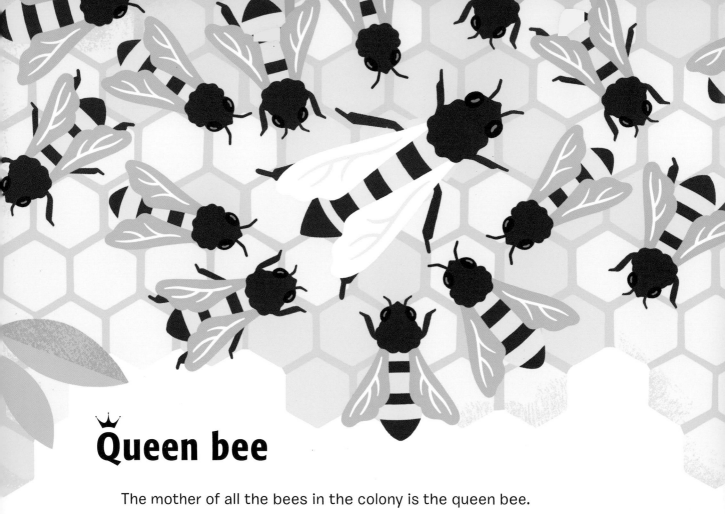

Queen bee

The mother of all the bees in the colony is the queen bee.
She is about twice as big as a worker bee.

The queen bee spends most of her life in the nest. Her worker
daughters bring her food and groom her. In winter, they
huddle around their queen to keep her warm. In summer,
they fan their wings to keep her cool.

A queen can live between 4 and 7 years, the longest of
any bee. The worker bee will survive for only 45 days,
while a drone can live twice as long.

The queen lays all the eggs for the colony.

Sometimes she lays as many as 1,000 eggs in a day.
Each one sits in its own little part of the nest, called a cell.

Inside the nest

Wild honey bees make their nests in trees
or between rocks, but many bees also nest in
boxes called hives, which people build for them.

Wooden frames filled with lots of six-sided
wax cells hang down from the top of the
hive. There are eggs in some of these
cells. Others hold young bees
or stores of food.

The bees make the
wax from their bodies.
A group of wax cells is
called a comb.

New bees

Bee eggs hatch into small, wriggly
creatures called larvae. It takes 21 days
for a larva to grow into an adult bee.

At first, the growing bee is fed "royal jelly,"
a rich, sugary food, by the worker bees in the
nest. Later, it is fed pollen and honey from
the colony's food stores.

A growing queen bee gets special treatment.
She is fed royal jelly the whole time she is
growing up, which helps to prepare her for
a life of laying eggs.

First days

When a young bee is fully grown, she leaves the cell she has been living in. Her first job is to clean it, and other cells too. It's important the cells are cleaned so they are ready for the next group of larvae, or to store food.

When she is about three days old, the young bee
begins to feed the new larvae. Then, in the second
week of life, her job changes. She starts building and
repairing the nest and making new wax cells.

Working in the hive

When she is about three weeks old, the bee starts another new job. She waits near the entrance of the hive, ready to take pollen and nectar from other bees flying home who have been collecting it.

She also guards the entrance, checking that all the returning bees are from her family and are not looking to steal honey. Guard bees can tell if bees are from other hives by their smell, and then they attack and chase them away.

Flying out

When a bee is about 22 days old, she is an adult
and ready to gather food. She does a few short
flights to practice flying and to learn to find
her way home. Then she flies out into the
open air to search for flowers.

The bee flies from plant to plant collecting nectar and pollen. Flower pollen is like yellow dust, and the bee carries it in parts of her back legs called pollen baskets. Nectar is a sweet liquid made by flowers. When the bee finds it, she sucks it up into an extra stomach called a honey sac.

Dancing bees

When a worker bee finds a patch of
flowers full of nectar and pollen, she
tells the other bees how to find it.
To do this, she does a dance.

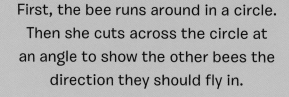

First, the bee runs around in a circle.
Then she cuts across the circle at
an angle to show the other bees the
direction they should fly in.

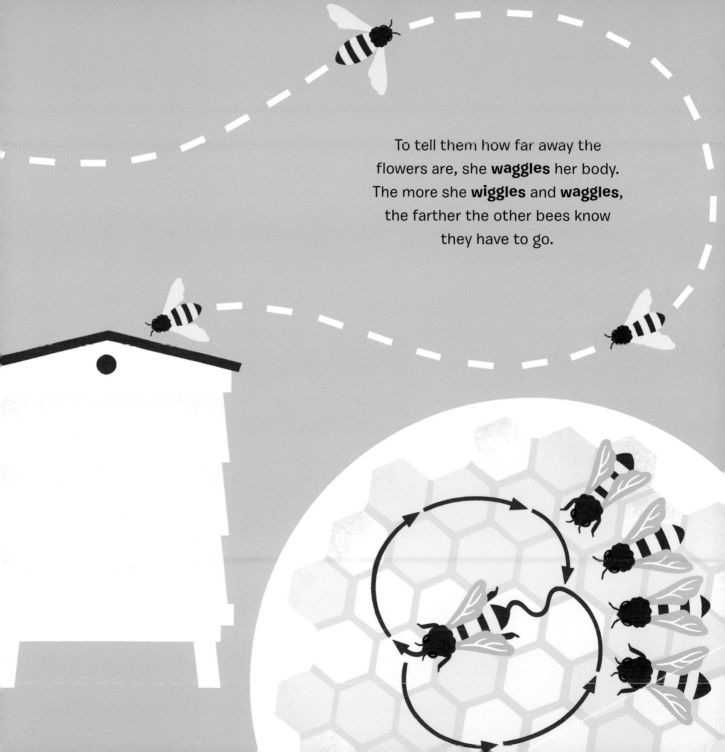

To tell them how far away the flowers are, she **waggles** her body. The more she **wiggles** and **waggles**, the farther the other bees know they have to go.

Flower to flower

Flowering plants need pollen from
a flower of the same kind to help
new plants grow.

Bees can help flowers get pollen. When a bee lands on a flower, its body gets covered in pollen. When it visits the next flower, some of this pollen brushes off and pollinates the plant.

Other insects, as well as birds and bats, pollinate flowers too, but bees are the most important pollinators. Without bees, many plants would not be able to produce seeds.

Making honey

Bees use nectar to make honey,
which they store in their hive until
it's time to eat.

A lot of work goes into making honey, so it's important for all the bees to work together. It takes about 10 million trips out from the nest to make enough honey to fill one jar.

Lots of other animals, including people, like to eat honey too, and they collect it from bees' nests. When people who keep bees do this, they always make sure they leave enough honey for the bees to eat.

A new nest

Sometimes, a bee colony gets too big.

When this happens, the queen may leave the
nest with all the older workers and drones
in a big group called a swarm.

Workers called scouts look for a place
to make a new nest. When they have
found one, their queen and the
other bees join them.

In the old nest, a new queen hatches.
She mates with drones from other hives
and starts to lay eggs to build up the
colony again.

Beekeeping

We need bees to pollinate our plants, and we love the honey that they make, but bees don't need humans. Wild bees can build their own nests.

We can, though, provide bees with a cozy hive-home, and in return take some of their honey. During the summer months, bees make more honey than they need.

When looking in the hive, a beekeeper must wear protective clothing and be very careful. Bees are not dangerous, but they will defend the hive.

A beekeeper's job is to look after the bees and watch for any signs of disease while disturbing the hive as little as possible.

Save the bees

Honey bees are in trouble. There's much less grassland and far fewer wildflower meadows than ever before, so it's harder for bees to gather the nectar and pollen they need. Bees are also harmed by the chemicals that farmers spray on their fields to kill other bugs.

You and your family can help by planting flowers in your garden and leaving wild spaces, or by planting seeds in areas of wasteland to make bee-friendly spaces. Buy local honey to support the beekeepers in your area, and tell people how important bees are to all of us.

Bees matter, and the more people speak up for them, the more likely it is that they will be protected.

Glossary

cell: A small compartment within the bees' hive

groom: To clean the hair or skin of another creature

insect: A small creature with six legs and one or two pairs of wings

larva: A newly hatched bee. Many larva are called larvae

mate: Two adult creatures coming together to create offspring

nectar: A sweet substance produced by flowers to attract bees, insects, and birds

pollen: Sticky yellow dust produced by flowers

pollinate: To spread pollen from one plant to another of the same kind so that it can reproduce

 # Find out more

If you would like to learn more about bees, here are some books and websites that can help you:

Bee: Nature's Tiny Miracle by Patricia Hegarty and Britta Teckentrup (Little Tiger Kids, 2016)

The Bee Book by Emma Tennant and Fergus Chadwick (Dorling Kindersley, 2016)

The Book of Bees by Piotr Socha and Wojciech Grajkowski (Thames and Hudson, 2016)

The website of the **Bumblebee Conservation Trust** has lots of information about bees and about how you can help them. Also, there are lots of activities and games in the Bumble Kids section: http://bumblebeeconservation.org/.

Find out all about bees in cities at www.beecityusa.org.

The Honeybee Conservancy has a campaign dedicated to protecting bees. You can find out all about it at thehoneybeeconservancy.org/sponsor-a-hive/.